What Is a Democracy?

by Jennifer Boothroyd

first step nonfiction

Lerner Publications ◆ Minneapolis

LERNER

e

SOURCE™

Expand learning beyond the printed book. Download free, complementary educational resources for this book from our website, www.lernerresource.com.

The images in this book are used with the permission of: © Mark Wilson/Getty Images, p. 4; © iStockphoto.com/Jani Bryson, p. 5; © iStockphoto.com/TommL, p. 6; Photoshot/Newscom, p. 7; Aaron Ufumeli/Newscom, p. 8; © iStockphoto.com/jameslee999, p. 9; © Nosnibor137/Bigstock.com, p. 10; © Hill Street Studios/Blend Images/Getty Images, p. 11; © David R. Frazier Photolibrary, Inc./Alamy, p. 12; CJ Gunther/EPA/Newscom, p. 13; © White House Photo/Alamy, p. 14; © J Burleson/Alamy, p. 15; © iStockphoto.com/BasSlabbers, p. 17; © Toronto Star/Getty Images, p. 17; © Robert E Daemmrich/The Image Bank/Getty Images, p. 18; © Dirk Anschutz/Stone/Getty Images, p. 19; © iStockphoto.com/4774344sean, p. 20; © iStockphoto.com/Mark Bowden, p. 21; © Bill Bachmann/Alamy, p. 22.

Front cover: © Richard Hutchings/CORBIS

Main body text set in ITC Avant Garde Gothic Std Medium 21/25.
Typeface provided by Adobe Systems.

Lerner Publications Company
A division of Lerner Publishing Group, Inc.
241 First Avenue North
Minneapolis, MN 55401 USA

For reading levels and more information, look up this title at www.lernerbooks.com.

Library of Congress Cataloging-in-Publication Data

Boothroyd, Jennifer, 1972–
        What is a democracy? / by Jennifer Boothroyd.
            pages cm. — (First step nonfiction - exploring government)
        Includes index.
        ISBN 978-1-4677-8574-7 (lb : alk. paper) — ISBN 978-1-4677-8621-8 (pb : alk. paper) — ISBN 978-1-4677-8622-5 (eb pdf)
        1. Democracy—Juvenile literature. I. Title.
JC423.B635 2015
321.8—dc23   2014044199

Manufactured in the United States of America
1 – CG – 7/15/15

Table of Contents

Types of Government

A **government** is a group
of people who run a
country.

People living in a country are called **citizens**.

Each country has a government.

There are many types of governments in the world.

Some countries are ruled
by a king or a queen.

Dictators make decisions for everyone.

Other countries are ruled by a **dictator**.

The United States is a **democracy**.

The citizens rule the country.

The people **elect** their leaders.

Citizens **vote** for the people who make rules.

Citizens choose the president.

Leaders take turns having power.

Citizens voted to build this school.

People can vote for a law or a project too.

People are free to share
their ideas.

People tell leaders what they think.

Each person has a say.

Leaders try to be fair to everyone.

You have a say in a democracy too.

This family voted on which movie to watch.

You can help your family choose a movie.

You can write an e-mail to a leader.

You can tell leaders what you think.

You can help elect a class president.

Glossary

citizens – people who live in a country or a state

democracy – a government run by leaders chosen by the people

dictator – one person or small group who rules a country

elect – to choose

government – the people in charge of a city, a state, or a country

vote – to make a choice in an election

Index